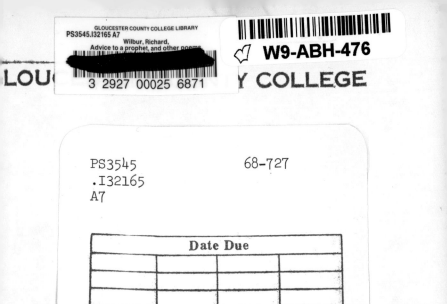

Date Due			

ADVICE TO A PROPHET

and other poems

BY THE SAME AUTHOR

The Beautiful Changes & other poems

Ceremony & other poems

A Bestiary (editor)

Molière's Misanthrope (translator)

Molière's Tartuffe (translator)

Things of This World (poems)

Poems 1943–1956

Poe: Complete Poems (editor)

Richard Wilbur
Advice to a Prophet
and other poems

HARCOURT, BRACE & WORLD, INC. NEW YORK

Of the poems in this book,
sixteen appeared originally in *The New Yorker;*
others appeared in *The American Scholar, Atlantic Monthly,*
Between Worlds, Chicago Choice, The Nation,
Partisan Review, Poetry, Quagga, and *Transatlantic Review.*

LIBRARY OF CONGRESS CATALOG CARD NUMBER: 61-15813
PRINTED IN THE UNITED STATES OF AMERICA

FOR LILLIAN HELLMAN

CONTENTS

ADVICE TO A PROPHET

and other poems

TWO VOICES IN A MEADOW

A Milkweed

Anonymous as cherubs
Over the crib of God,
White seeds are floating
Out of my burst pod.
What power had I
Before I learned to yield?
Shatter me, great wind:
I shall possess the field.

A Stone

As casual as cow-dung
Under the crib of God,
I lie where chance would have me,
Up to the ears in sod.
Why should I move? To move
Befits a light desire.
The sill of Heaven would founder,
Did such as I aspire.

ADVICE TO A PROPHET

When you come, as you soon must, to the streets of our city,
Mad-eyed from stating the obvious,
Not proclaiming our fall but begging us
In God's name to have self-pity,

Spare us all word of the weapons, their force and range,
The long numbers that rocket the mind;
Our slow, unreckoning hearts will be left behind,
Unable to fear what is too strange.

Nor shall you scare us with talk of the death of the race.
How should we dream of this place without us?—
The sun mere fire, the leaves untroubled about us,
A stone look on the stone's face?

Speak of the world's own change. Though we cannot conceive
Of an undreamt thing, we know to our cost
How the dreamt cloud crumbles, the vines are blackened
        by frost,
How the view alters. We could believe,

If you told us so, that the white-tailed deer will slip
Into perfect shade, grown perfectly shy,
The lark avoid the reaches of our eye,
The jack-pine lose its knuckled grip

On the cold ledge, and every torrent burn
As Xanthus once, its gliding trout
Stunned in a twinkling. What should we be without
The dolphin's arc, the dove's return,

These things in which we have seen ourselves and spoken?
Ask us, prophet, how we shall call
Our natures forth when that live tongue is all
Dispelled, that glass obscured or broken

In which we have said the rose of our love and the clean
Horse of our courage, in which beheld
The singing locust of the soul unshelled,
And all we mean or wish to mean.

Ask us, ask us whether with the worldless rose
Our hearts shall fail us; come demanding
Whether there shall be lofty or long standing
When the bronze annals of the oak-tree close.

STOP

In grimy winter dusk
We slowed for a concrete platform;
The pillars passed more slowly;
A paper bag leapt up.

The train banged to a standstill.
Brake-steam rose and parted.
Three chipped-at blocks of ice
Sprawled on a baggage-truck.

Out in that glum, cold air
The broken ice lay glintless,
But the truck was painted blue
On side, wheels, and tongue,

A purple, glowering blue
Like the phosphorus of Lethe
Or Queen Persephone's gaze
In the numb fields of the dark.

JUNK

Huru Welandes
                    worc ne geswiceð
monna ænigum
                    ðara ðe Mimming can
heardne gehealdan.

WALDERE

An axe angles
                    from my neighbor's ashcan;
It is hell's handiwork,
                    the wood not hickory,
The flow of the grain
                    not faithfully followed.
The shivered shaft
                    rises from a shellheap
Of plastic playthings,
                    paper plates,
And the sheer shards
                    of shattered tumblers
That were not annealed
                    for the time needful.
At the same curbside,
                    a cast-off cabinet
Of wavily-warped
                    unseasoned wood
Waits to be trundled
                    in the trash-man's truck.

Haul them off! Hide them!

                      The heart winces

For junk and gimcrack,

                for jerrybuilt things

And the men who make them

                  for a little money,

Bartering pride

            like the bought boxer

Who pulls his punches,

               or the paid-off jockey

Who in the home stretch

              holds in his horse.

Yet the things themselves

              in thoughtless honor

Have kept composure,

            like captives who would not

Talk under torture.

            Tossed from a tailgate

Where the dump displays

             its random dolmens,

Its black barrows

           and blazing valleys,

They shall waste in the weather

               toward what they were.

The sun shall glory

          in the glitter of glass-chips,

Foreseeing the salvage

          of the prisoned sand,

And the blistering paint

          peel off in patches,

That the good grain

        be discovered again.

Then burnt, bulldozed,

                    they shall all be buried

To the depth of diamonds,

                       in the making dark

Where halt Hephaestus

                    keeps his hammer

And Wayland's work

               is worn away.

LOVES OF THE PUPPETS

Meeting when all the world was in the bud,
Drawn each to each by instinct's wooden face,
These lovers, heedful of the mystic blood,
Fell glassy-eyed into a hot embrace.

April, unready to be so intense,
Marked time while these outstripped the gentle weather,
Yielded their natures to insensate sense,
And flew apart the more they came together.

Where did they fly? Why, each through such a storm
As may be conjured in a globe of glass
Drove on the colder as the flesh grew warm,
In breathless haste to be at lust's impasse,

To cross the little bridge and sink to rest
In visions of the snow-occluded house
Where languishes, unfound by any quest,
The perfect, small, asphyxiated spouse.

That blizzard ended, and their eyes grew clear,
And there they lay exhausted yet unsated;
Why did their features run with tear on tear,
Until their looks were individuated?

One peace implies another, and they cried
For want of love as if their souls would crack,
Till, in despair of being satisfied,
They vowed at least to share each other's lack.

Then maladroitly they embraced once more,
And hollow rang to hollow with a sound
That tuned the brooks more sweetly than before,
And made the birds explode for miles around.

A SUMMER MORNING

Her young employers, having got in late
From seeing friends in town
And scraped the right front fender on the gate,
Will not, the cook expects, be coming down.

She makes a quiet breakfast for herself.
The coffee-pot is bright,
The jelly where it should be on the shelf.
She breaks an egg into the morning light,

Then, with the bread-knife lifted, stands and hears
The sweet efficient sounds
Of thrush and catbird, and the snip of shears
Where, in the terraced backward of the grounds,

A gardener works before the heat of day.
He straightens for a view
Of the big house ascending stony-gray
Out of his beds mosaic with the dew.

His young employers having got in late,
He and the cook alone
Receive the morning on their old estate,
Possessing what the owners can but own.

A HOLE IN THE FLOOR

for René Magritte

The carpenter's made a hole
In the parlor floor, and I'm standing
Staring down into it now
At four o'clock in the evening,
As Schliemann stood when his shovel
Knocked on the crowns of Troy.

A clean-cut sawdust sparkles
On the grey, shaggy laths,
And here is a cluster of shavings
From the time when the floor was laid.
They are silvery-gold, the color
Of Hesperian apple-parings.

Kneeling, I look in under
Where the joists go into hiding.
A pure street, faintly littered
With bits and strokes of light,
Enters the long darkness
Where its parallels will meet.

The radiator-pipe
Rises in middle distance
Like a shuttered kiosk, standing
Where the only news is night.
Here it's not painted green,
As it is in the visible world.

For God's sake, what am I after?
Some treasure, or tiny garden?
Or that untrodden place,
The house's very soul,
Where time has stored our footbeats
And the long skein of our voices?

Not these, but the buried strangeness
Which nourishes the known:
That spring from which the floor-lamp
Drinks now a wilder bloom,
Inflaming the damask love-seat
And the whole dangerous room.

Jorge Guillén: THE HORSES

Shaggy and heavily natural, they stand
Immobile under their thick and cumbrous **manes,**
Pent in a barbed enclosure which contains,
By way of compensation, grazing-land.

Nothing disturbs them now. In slow increase
They fatten like the grass. Doomed to be idle,
To haul no cart or wagon, wear no bridle,
They grow into a vegetable peace.

Soul is the issue of so strict a fate.
They harbor visions in their waking eyes,
And with their quiet ears participate
In heaven's pure serenity, which lies
So near all things—yet from the beasts **concealed.**
Serene now, superhuman, they crop their field.

Jorge Guillén: DEATH, FROM A DISTANCE

Je soutenais l'éclat
de la mort toute pure.
VALÉRY

When that dead-certainty appals my thought,
My future trembles on the road ahead.
There where the light of country fields is caught
In the blind, final precinct of the dead,
A wall takes aim.
              But what is sad, stripped bare
By the sun's gaze? It does not matter now,—
Not yet. What matters is the ripened pear
That even now my hand strips from the bough.

The time will come: my hand will reach, some day,
Without desire. That saddest day of all,
I shall not weep, but with a proper awe
For the great force impending, I shall say,
Lay on, just destiny. Let the white wall
Impose on me its uncapricious law.

SHE

What was her beauty in our first estate
When Adam's will was whole, and the least thing
Appeared the gift and creature of his king,
How should we guess? Resemblance had to wait

For separation, and in such a place
She so partook of water, light, and trees
As not to look like any one of these.
He woke and gazed into her naked face.

But then she changed, and coming down amid
The flocks of Abel and the fields of Cain,
Clothed in their wish, her Eden graces hid,
A shape of plenty with a mop of grain,

She broke upon the world, in time took on
The look of every labor and its fruits.
Columnar in a robe of pleated lawn
She cupped her patient hand for attributes,

Was radiant captive of the farthest tower
And shed her honor on the fields of war,
Walked in her garden at the evening hour,
Her shadow like a dark ogival door,

Breasted the seas for all the westward ships
And, come to virgin country, changed again—
A moonlike being truest in eclipse,
And subject goddess of the dreams of men.

Tree, temple, valley, prow, gazelle, machine,
More named and nameless than the morning star,
Lovely in every shape, in all unseen,
We dare not wish to find you as you are,

Whose apparition, biding time until
Desire decay and bring the latter age,
Shall flourish in the ruins of our will
And deck the broken stones like saxifrage.

GEMINI

I

Because poor PUER's both unsure and vain,
Those who befriend him suffer his disdain,
While those who snub him gain his deference.
He loves his enemies, in a certain sense.

II

It is the power of Heaven to withdraw
Which fills PUELLA with religious awe.
She worships the remoteness of a wraith.
If God should die for her, she'd lose her faith.

THE UNDEAD

Even as children they were late sleepers,
Preferring their dreams, even when quick with monsters,
    To the world with all its breakable toys,
        Its compacts with the dying;

From the stretched arms of withered trees
They turned, fearing contagion of the mortal,
    And even under the plums of summer
        Drifted like winter moons.

Secret, unfriendly, pale, possessed
Of the one wish, the thirst for mere survival,
    They came, as all extremists do
        In time, to a sort of grandeur:

Now, to their Balkan battlements
Above the vulgar town of their first lives,
    They rise at the moon's rising. Strange
        That their utter self-concern

Should, in the end, have left them selfless:
Mirrors fail to perceive them as they float
    Through the great hall and up the staircase;
        Nor are the cobwebs broken.

Into the pallid night emerging,
Wrapped in their flapping capes, routinely maddened
    By a wolf's cry, they stand for a moment
        Stoking the mind's eye

With lewd thoughts of the pressed flowers
And bric-a-brac of rooms with something to lose,—
Of love-dismembered dolls, and children
Buried in quilted sleep.

Then they are off in a negative frenzy,
Their black shapes cropped into sudden bats
That swarm, burst, and are gone. Thinking
Of a thrush cold in the leaves

Who has sung his few summers truly,
Or an old scholar resting his eyes at last,
We cannot be much impressed with vampires,
Colorful though they are;

Nevertheless, their pain is real,
And requires our pity. Think how sad it must be
To thirst always for a scorned elixir,
The salt quotidian blood

Which, if mistrusted, has no savor;
To prey on life forever and not possess it,
As rock-hollows, tide after tide,
Glassily strand the sea.

OCTOBER MAPLES, PORTLAND

The leaves, though little time they have to live,
Were never so unfallen as today,
And seem to yield us through a rustled sieve
The very light from which time fell away.

A showered fire we thought forever lost
Redeems the air. Where friends in passing meet,
They parley in the tongues of Pentecost.
Gold ranks of temples flank the dazzled street.

It is a light of maples, and will go;
But not before it washes eye and brain
With such a tincture, such a sanguine glow
As cannot fail to leave a lasting stain.

So Mary's laundered mantle (in the tale
Which, like all pretty tales, may still be true),
Spread on the rosemary-bush, so drenched the pale
Slight blooms in its irradiated hue,

They could not choose but to return in blue.

EIGHT RIDDLES FROM SYMPHOSIUS

I

Hung from a foot, I walk upon my head,
And leave a trail of headprints where I tread!
Yet many of my kind are thus bestead.

II

I have borne more than a body ought to bear.
Three souls I harbored; when I lost a pair,
The third one all but perished then and there.

III

I bite, when bitten; but because I lack
For teeth, no biter scruples to attack,
And many bite me to be bitten back.

IV

Unequal in degree, alike in size,
We make our flight, ascending toward the skies,
And rise with those who by our help can rise.

V

Mine was the strangest birth under the sun;
I left the womb, yet life had not begun;
Entered the world, and yet was seen by none.

VI

Sweet purlings in an earth-walled inn resound.
Within that inn a silent guest is found.
Together, guest and inn are onward bound.

VII

All teeth from head to foot (yet friend to men),
I rip and tear my green-haired prey; but then,
All that I chew I spew right out again.

VIII

To me, and through me, Fortune is unkind.
Though iron-bound, yet many must I bind—
And many free, though I remain confined.

SHAME

It is a cramped little state with no foreign policy,
Save to be thought inoffensive. The grammar of the
    language
Has never been fathomed, owing to the national habit
Of allowing each sentence to trail off in confusion.
Those who have visited Scusi, the capital city,
Report that the railway-route from Schuldig passes
Through country best described as unrelieved.
Sheep are the national product. The faint inscription
Over the city gates may perhaps be rendered,
"I'm afraid you won't find much of interest here."
Census-reports which give the population
As zero are, of course, not to be trusted,
Save as reflecting the natives' flustered insistence
That they do not count, as well as their modest horror
Of letting one's sex be known in so many words.
The uniform grey of the nondescript buildings, the
    absence
Of churches or comfort-stations, have given observers
An odd impression of ostentatious meanness,
And it must be said of the citizens (muttering by
In their ratty sheepskins, shying at cracks in the sidewalk)
That they lack the peace of mind of the truly humble.
The tenor of life is careful, even in the stiff
Unsmiling carelessness of the border-guards
And *douaniers*, who admit, whenever they can,
Not merely the usual carloads of deodorant
But gypsies, g-strings, hasheesh, and contraband pigments.

Their complete negligence is reserved, however,
For the hoped-for invasion, at which time the happy people
(Sniggering, ruddily naked, and shamelessly drunk)
Will stun the foe by their overwhelming submission,
Corrupt the generals, infiltrate the staff,
Usurp the throne, proclaim themselves to be sun-gods,
And bring about the collapse of the whole empire.

A GRASSHOPPER

But for a brief
Moment, a poised minute,
He paused on the chicory-leaf;
Yet within it

The sprung perch
Had time to absorb the shock,
Narrow its pitch and lurch,
Cease to rock.

A quiet spread
Over the neighbor ground;
No flower swayed its head
For yards around;

The wind shrank
Away with a swallowed hiss;
Caught in a widening, blank
Parenthesis,

Cry upon cry
Faltered and faded out;
Everything seemed to die.
Oh, without doubt

Peace like a plague
Had gone to the world's verge,
But that an aimless, vague
Grasshopper-urge

Leapt him aloft,
Giving the leaf a kick,
Starting the grasses' soft
Chafe and tick,

So that the sleeping
Crickets resumed their chimes,
And all things wakened, keeping
Their several times.

In gay release
The whole field did what it did,
Peaceful now that its peace
Lay busily hid.

Salvatore Quasimodo:

THE AGRIGENTUM ROAD

That wind's still there that I remember afire
In the manes of the racing horses
Veering across the plains; a wind
That stains the sandstone and erodes the hearts
Of downed columnar statues in the grass.
Oh antique soul, bled white
By rancor, back you lean to that wind again,
Catching the delicate fetor of the moss
That clothes those giants tumbled down by heaven.
How lonely it will be, the time that is left you!
    Worse, worse, if you should hear
That sound again, borne toward the far-off sea
Which Hesperus already pinks with morning:
The jew's-harp quavering sadly in the mouth
Of the wagon-maker climbing
Slowly his moon-washed hill, amidst
The murmur of the Saracen olive trees.

THE ASPEN AND THE STREAM

The Aspen

Beholding element, in whose pure eye
My boughs upon a ground of heaven lie—
O deep surrendered mind, where cloud and stone
Compose their beings and efface your own,
Teach me, like you, to drink creation whole
And, casting out my self, become a soul.

The Stream

Why should the water drink,
Blithering little tree?
Think what you choose to think,
But lisp no more at me.

I seek an empty mind.
Reflection is my curse.
Oh, never have I been blind
To the damned universe,

Save when I rose in flood
And in my lathered flight
So fouled myself with mud
As to be purged of sight.

The Aspen

Your water livens me, but not your word,
If what you spoke was what I thought I heard.
But likely I mistook you. What with the claims
Of crow and cricket teaching me their names,
And all this flap and shifting in my head,
I must have lost the drift of what you said.

The Stream

There may be rocks ahead
Where, shivered into smoke
And brawling in my bed,
I'll shred this gaudy cloak;

Then, dodging down a trough
Into a rocky hole,
I'll shake the daylight off
And repossess my soul

In blackness and in fall,
Where self to self shall roar
Till, deaf and blind to all,
I shall be self no more.

The Aspen

Out of your sullen flux I shall distil
A gayer spirit and a clambering will,
And reach toward all about me, and ensnare
With roots the earth, with branches all the air—
Even if that blind groping but achieves
A darker head, a few more aspen-leaves.

A FIRE-TRUCK

Right down the shocked street with a siren-blast
That sends all else skittering to the curb,
Redness, brass, ladders and hats hurl past,
    Blurring to sheer verb,

Shift at the corner into uproarious gear
And make it around the turn in a squall of traction,
The headlong bell maintaining sure and clear,
    Thought is degraded action!

Beautiful, heavy, unweary, loud, obvious thing!
I stand here purged of nuance, my mind a blank.
All I was brooding upon has taken wing,
    And I have you to thank.

As you howl beyond hearing I carry you into my mind,
Ladders and brass and all, there to admire
Your phoenix-red simplicity, enshrined
    In that not extinguished fire.

Even when first her face,
Younger than any spring,
Older than Pharaoh's grain
And fresh as Phoenix-ashes,
5 Shadowed under its lashes
Every earthly thing,
There was another place
I saw in a flash of pain:
Off in the fathomless dark
10 Beyond the verge of love
I saw blind fishes move,
And under a stone shelf
Rode the recusant shark—
Cold, waiting, himself.

15 Oh, even when we fell,
Clean as a mountain source
And barely able to tell
Such ecstasy from grace,
Into the primal bed
20 And current of our race,
We knew yet must deny
To what we gathered head:
That music growing harsh,
Trees blotting the sky
25 Above the roaring course
That in the summer's drought
Slowly would peter out
Into a dry marsh.

Love is the greatest mercy,
30   A volley of the sun
That lashes all with shade,
That the first day be mended;
And yet, so soon undone,
It is the lover's curse
35   Till time be comprehended
And the flawed heart unmade.
What can I do but move
From folly to defeat,
And call that sorrow sweet
40   That teaches us to see
The final face of love
In what we cannot be?

IN THE SMOKING-CAR

The eyelids meet. He'll catch a little nap.
The grizzled, crew-cut head drops to his chest.
It shakes above the briefcase on his lap.
Close voices breathe, "Poor sweet, he did his best."

"Poor sweet, poor sweet," the bird-hushed glades repeat,
Through which in quiet pomp his litter goes,
Carried by native girls with naked feet.
A sighing stream concurs in his repose.

Could he but think, he might recall to mind
The righteous mutiny or sudden gale
That beached him here; the dear ones left behind . . .
So near the ending, he forgets the tale.

Were he to lift his eyelids now, he might
Behold his maiden porters, brown and bare.
But even here he has no appetite.
It is enough to know that they are there.

Enough that now a honeyed music swells,
The gentle, mossed declivities begin,
And the whole air is full of flower-smells.
Failure, the longed-for valley, takes him in.

BALLADE FOR THE
DUKE OF ORLÉANS

*who offered a prize at Blois, circa 1457, for
the best ballade employing the line "Je
meurs de soif auprès de la fontaine."*

Flailed from the heart of water in a bow,
He took the falling fly; my line went taut;
Foam was in uproar where he drove below;
In spangling air I fought him and was fought.
Then, wearied to the shallows, he was caught,
Gasped in the net, lay still and stony-eyed.
It was no fading iris I had sought.
I die of thirst, here at the fountain-side.

Down in the harbor's flow and counter-flow
I left my ships with hopes and heroes fraught.
Ten times more golden than the sun could show,
Calypso gave the darkness I besought.
Oh, but her fleecy touch was dearly bought:
All spent, I wakened by my only bride,
Beside whom every vision is but nought,
And die of thirst, here at the fountain-side.

Where does that Plenty dwell, I'd like to know,
Which fathered poor Desire, as Plato taught?
Out on the real and endless waters go
Conquistador and stubborn Argonaut.
Where Buddha bathed, the golden bowl he brought
Gilded the stream, but stalled its living tide.
The sunlight withers as the verse is wrought.
I die of thirst, here at the fountain-side.

Duke, keep your coin. All men are born distraught,
And will not for the world be satisfied.
Whether we live in fact, or but in thought,
We die of thirst, here at the fountain-side.

Gérard de Nerval: *A N T E R O S*

You ask me why I bear such rage in heart,
And on this pliant neck a rebel head;
Of great Antaeus' lineage was I bred;
I hurl to heaven again the Victor's dart.

Yea, I am one the Avenger God inspires;
He has marked my forehead with the breath of spite;
My face, like Abel's bloody—alas!—and white,
Burns red by turns with Cain's unsated fires!

The last, Jehovah! who by thy powers fell
And cried against thy tyranny from hell
Was Bel my grandsire, or my father Dagon.

By them thrice baptized in Cocytus' water,
I guard alone the Amalekite my mother,
And sow at her feet the teeth of the old dragon.

TO ISHTAR

Is it less than your brilliance, Ishtar,
How the snowfield smarts in the fresh sun,
And the bells of its melting ring, and we blink
At the light flexing in trickles?

It is the Spring's disgrace
That already, before the prone arbutus
Will risk its whiteness, you have come down
To the first gate and darkened.

Forgive us, who cannot conceive you
Elsewhere and maiden, but love you only
Fallen among us in rut and furrow,
In the shade of amassing leaves,

Or scrawny in plucked harvest,
Your losses having fattened the world
Till crownless, starless, you stoop and enter
The low door of Irkalla.

There too, in the year's dungeon
Where love takes you, even our itch
For defilement cannot find you out,
Your death being so perfect.

It is all we can do to witness
The waste motions of empty trees,
The joyless tittering duff, the grass-mats
Blanched and scurfy with ice,

And in the desert heat
Of vision force from rotten sticks
Those pure and inconceivable blooms
Which, rising, you bear beyond us.

PANGLOSS'S SONG: A Comic-Opera Lyric

I

Dear boy, you will not hear me speak
    With sorrow or with rancor
Of what has paled my rosy cheek
    And blasted it with canker;
'Twas Love, great Love, that did the deed
    Through Nature's gentle laws,
And how should ill effects proceed
    From so divine a cause?

Sweet honey comes from bees that sting,
    As you are well aware;
To one adept in reasoning,
Whatever pains disease may bring
Are but the tangy seasoning
    To Love's delicious fare.

II

Columbus and his men, they say,
    Conveyed the virus hither
Whereby my features rot away
    And vital powers wither;
Yet had they not traversed the seas
    And come infected back,

Why, think of all the luxuries
    That modern life would lack!

All bitter things conduce to sweet,
    As this example shows;
Without the little spirochete
We'd have no chocolate to eat,
Nor would tobacco's fragrance greet
    The European nose.

III

Each nation guards its native land
    With cannon and with sentry,
Inspectors look for contraband
    At every port of entry,
Yet nothing can prevent the spread
    Of Love's divine disease:
It rounds the world from bed to bed
    As pretty as you please.

Men worship Venus everywhere,
    As plainly may be seen;
The decorations which I bear
Are nobler than the Croix de Guerre,
And gained in service of our fair
    And universal Queen.

TWO QUATRAINS FOR FIRST FROST

I

Hot summer has exhausted her intent
To the last rose and roundelay and seed.
No leaf has changed, and yet these leaves now read
Like a love-letter that's no longer meant.

II

Now on all things is the dull restive mood
Of some rich gambler who in quick disdain
Plumps all on zero, hoping so to gain
Fresh air, light pockets, and his solitude.

ANOTHER VOICE

The sword bites for peace,
Yet how should that be said
Now or in howling Greece
Above the sorry dead?
Corcyra! cry the crows,
And blacken all our sky.
The soul knows what it knows,
But may not make reply.

From a good face gone mad,
From false or hissing tongue,
What comfort's to be had,
What sweetness can be wrung?
It is the human thing
To reckon pain as pain.
If soul in quiet sing,
Better not to explain.

Great martyrs mocked their pain
And sang that wrong was right;
Great doctors proved them sane
By logic's drier light;
Yet in those I love the most
Some anger, love, or tact
Hushes the giddy ghost
Before atrocious fact.

Forgive me, patient voice
Whose word I little doubt,
Who stubbornly rejoice
When all but beaten out,
If I equivocate,
And will not yet unlearn
Anxiety and hate,
Sorrow and dear concern.

ORGON, CLÉANTE, DORINE

ORGON
                              Ah, Brother, good-day.

CLÉANTE
Well, welcome back. I'm sorry I can't stay.
How was the country? Blooming, I trust, and green?

ORGON
Excuse me, Brother; just one moment. (*to Dorine:*) Dorine . . .
        (*to Cléante:*)
To put my mind at rest, I always learn
The household news the moment I return.
        (*to Dorine:*)
Has all been well, these two days I've been gone?
How are the family? What's been going on?

DORINE
Your wife, two days ago, had a bad fever,
And a fierce headache that refused to leave her.

ORGON
Ah. And Tartuffe?

DORINE
                              Tartuffe? Why, he's round and red,
Bursting with health, and excellently fed.

ORGON
Poor devil!

DORINE

That night, the mistress was unable
To take a single bite at the dinner-table.
Her headache-pains, she said, were simply hellish.

ORGON

Ah. And Tartuffe?

DORINE

He ate his meal with relish,
And zealously devoured in her presence
A leg of mutton and a brace of pheasants.

ORGON

Poor devil!

DORINE

Well, the pains continued strong,
And so she tossed and tossed the whole night long,—
Now icy-cold, now burning like a flame.
We sat beside her bed till morning came.

ORGON

Ah. And Tartuffe?

DORINE

Why, having eaten, he rose
And sought his room, already in a doze,
Got into his warm bed, and snored away
In perfect peace until the break of day.

ORGON

Poor devil!

DORINE

After much ado, we talked her
Into dispatching someone for the doctor.
He bled her, and the fever quickly fell.

ORGON

Ah. And Tartuffe?

DORINE

He bore it very well.
To keep his cheerfulness at any cost,
And make up for the blood *Madame* had lost,
He drank, at lunch, four beakers full of port.

ORGON

Poor devil!

DORINE

Both are much improved, in short.
I'll go and tell *Madame* that you've expressed
Keen sympathy and anxious interest.

FALL IN CORRALES

Winter will be feasts and fires in the shut houses,
Lovers with hot mouths in their blanched bed,
Prayers and poems made, and all recourses
Against the world huge and dead:

Charms, all charms, as in stillness of plumb summer
The shut head lies down in bottomless grasses,
Willing that its thought be all heat and hum,
That it not dream the time passes.

Now as these light buildings of summer begin
To crumble, the air husky with blown tile,
It is as when in bald April the wind
Unhoused the spirit for a while:

Then there was no need by tales or drowsing
To make the thing that we were mothered by;
It was ourselves who melted in the mountains,
And the sun dove into every eye.

Our desires dwelt in the weather as fine as bomb-dust;
It was our sex that made the fountains yield;
Our flesh fought in the roots, and at last rested
Whole among cows in the risen field.

Now in its empty bed the truant river
Leaves but the perfect rumples of its flow;
The cottonwoods are spending gold like water;
Weeds in their light detachments go;

In a dry world more huge than rhyme or dreaming
We hear the sentences of straws and stones,
Stand in the wind and, bowing to this time,
Practise the candor of our bones.

NEXT DOOR

The home for the aged opens its windows in May,
    And the stale voices of winter-long
Flap from their dusty curtains toward our wood,
      That now with robin-song

Rouses, and is regaled. Promptly the trees
    Break bud and startle into leaf,
Blotting the old from sight, while all the birds
      Repeal the winter's grief

Pitilessly, resolving every sigh
    Or quaver to a chipper trill,
And snaring the sick cough within the rapt
      Beat of the flicker's bill.

Must we not see or hear these worn and frail?
    They are such hearts, for all we know,
As will not cheat the world of their regard,
      Even as they let it go.

Seated, perhaps, along a shady porch
    In the calm, wicker stalls of age,
Old crones and played-out cronies, they project
      Upon a cloudy stage

Gossip of strong-man, dancer, priest, and all
    They knew who had the gift of life,
Artisan, lover, soldier, orator,
      Wild bitch and happy wife,

Lying the more as recollection fails,
    Until for their enchanted souls
The players are forgotten, and they see
      Only such naked rôles

As David was, or Helen, and invent
    Out of their fabulous memories
Alcestis climbing home again, with big
      Death-bullying Heracles.

Is it like this? We have no way to know.
    Our lawn is loud with girls and boys.
The leaves are full and busy with the sun.
      The birds make too much noise.

A CHRISTMAS HYMN

A stable-lamp is lighted
Whose glow shall wake the sky;
The stars shall bend their voices,
And every stone shall cry.
And every stone shall cry,
And straw like gold shall shine;
A barn shall harbor heaven,
A stall become a shrine.

This child through David's city
Shall ride in triumph by;
The palm shall strew its branches,
And every stone shall cry.
And every stone shall cry,
Though heavy, dull, and dumb,
And lie within the roadway
To pave his kingdom come.

Yet he shall be forsaken,
And yielded up to die;
The sky shall groan and darken,
And every stone shall cry.
And every stone shall cry
For stony hearts of men:
God's blood upon the spearhead,
God's love refused again.

But now, as at the ending,
The low is lifted high;
The stars shall bend their voices,
And every stone shall cry.
And every stone shall cry
In praises of the child
By whose descent among us
The worlds are reconciled.

NOTES

ADVICE TO A PROPHET: Hephaestus, invoked by Achilles, scalded the river Xanthus (Scamander) in *Iliad,* xxi.

JUNK: The epigraph, taken from a fragmentary Anglo-Saxon poem, concerns the legendary smith Wayland, and may roughly be translated: "Truly, Wayland's handiwork—the sword Mimming which he made—will never fail any man who knows how to use it bravely."

THE UNDEAD: The *Standard Dictionary of Folklore, Mythology, and Legend* defines the vampire as "One of the types of the un-dead; a living corpse or soulless body that comes from its burial place and drinks the blood of the living."

EIGHT RIDDLES FROM SYMPHOSIUS: The answers to these riddles of Symphosius (A.D. Fourth Century?) are as follows: I, hobnail; II, mother of twins; III, onion; IV, stairs; V, chick in the egg; VI, river and fish; VII, saw; VIII, chain or fetter.

A FIRE TRUCK: Line 8 echoes a notion entertained by Henry Adams in his "Letter to American Teachers of History" (1910).

*appetitivae partis, quae dicuntur morales, inquantum
sunt virtutes. Et propterea dicit Gregorius (Moral.
22, 1), quod ceterae virtutes, nisi ea quae appetunt,
prudenter agant, virtutes esse nequaquam possunt."*
Virt. comm. 6; cf. Quol. 12, 22.

11 3, d. 33, 2, 5.

12 *"Regula intellectualis virtutis (qua determinatur
medium virtutis moralis; I, II, 64, 3, obj. 2) . . .
est . . . ipsa res."* I, II, 64, 3 ad 2.

13 II, II, 49, 3.

14 *"Homo autem est multarum operationum et diver-
sarum; et hoc propter nobilitatem sui principii ac-
tivi, scil. animae, cuius virtus ad infinita quodam-
modo se extendit."* Virt. comm. 6.

15 *"Cum hoc (bonum proprium hominis) multipliciter
varietur et in multis bonum hominis consistat, non
potuit homini inesse naturalis appetitus huius boni
determinati, secundum condiciones omnes quae requiruntur ad hoc quod sit ei bonum, cum hoc
multipliciter varietur secundum diversas condiciones
personarum et temporum et locorum et huiusmodi.
. . . Ita oportet quod ratio practica perficiatur
aliquo habitu ad hoc quod recte diiudicet de bono
humano secundum singula agenda. Et haec virtus
dicitur prudentia."* Virt. comm. 6.

16 *"Unumquodque autem horum contingit multipliciter
fieri et non eodem modo in omnibus; unde ad hoc
quod rectus modus statuatur, requiritur iudicii prudentia."* Virt. comm. 6.

17 *"Ea quae sunt ad finem in rebus humanis non sunt*

determinata, sed multipliciter diversificantur secun-
dum diversitatem personarum et negotiorum." II,
II, 47, 15; cf. Virt. comm. 13 ad 17; II, II, 47, 2
ad 3.

18 "Every mean of moral virtue is a rational mean,
since moral virtue is said to observe the mean,
through conformity with right reason. But it hap-
pens sometimes that the rational mean is also the
real mean; in which case the mean of moral virtue
is the real mean, for instance, in justice. On the
other hand, sometimes the rational mean is not
the real mean, but is considered in relation to us:
and such is the mean in all the other moral virtues.
The reason for this is that justice is about opera-
tions, which deal with external things, wherein the
right has to be established simply and absolutely.
Therefore the rational mean in justice gives to
each one his due, neither more nor less. But the
other moral virtues deal with interior passions,
wherein the right cannot be established in the same
way, since men are variously situated in relation
to their passions; hence the rectitude of reason has
to be established in the passions, with due regard
to us, who are moved in respect to the passions"
(I, II, 54, 2). "The other moral virtues are chiefly
concerned with the passions, the regulation of which
is gauged entirely by relation with the very man
who is the subject of those passions, in so far as
his anger and desire are vested with their various
due circumstances. Hence the mean in such virtues

is measured not by the proportion of one thing to another, but merely by comparison with the virtuous man himself, so that with them the mean is only that which is fixed by reason with regard to ourselves" (II, II, 58, 10; cf. I, II, 60, 2; II, II, 61, 2 ad 1).

19 This is, of course, not intended to justify extreme subjectivism in personal decision, nor to deny the unconditional validity of general moral standards. Primarily, prudence means not leaving a decision to purely subjective feeling for values, but requiring the subject to act by the objective standard of reality. Furthermore, as we have noted, the essence of prudence is that it is directed toward the *means,* not toward the end; we have seen also that for prudence to act at all presupposes the dictates of the innate conscience (synderesis). Prudence includes synderesis. The innate conscience, however, is nothing else than the presence in the mind of the natural moral law; that is to say, speaking more specifically, of God's Ten Commandments. Therefore anything that contradicts the natural moral law can never —in *no* "concrete situation"—be prudent and good. Finally, as we have likewise indicated, the obligations of justice in the proper sense are to a particular degree independent of situation. Cf. in this connection what has been cited in connection with note 18.

The doctrine of prudence is no more and no less "subjectivistic" than the general Christian teaching

that man is not allowed to act against his conscience (Rom. 14, 23), not even if this conscience
be mistaken.

Above all, however, it is necessary to say that
precisely the omission of special dictates for moral
behavior distinguishes Christianity from Judaism,
the period *post Christum natum* from the period
ante Christum natum. Extreme casuistry has rightly
been termed "Judaistic" (Linsenmann; cf. note 27)
and "Talmudistic" (Hirscher; cf. note 27). The
Law of the New Covenant is, as Thomas says in
harmony with the Epistle of James (1, 25), "the
law of perfect freedom"; "the Old Law, on the
contrary, determined many things and left but little
to be determined by human freedom" (I, II, 108,
1). "The New Law had no need to establish, by
commandments and injunctions, any other external
acts than the sacraments and the Commandments
which in themselves belong to the essence of virtue,
such as that we shall not kill, or steal, and other
commandments of this sort" (I, II, 108, 2).

20 II, II, 47, 3.

21 Cf. note 15.

22 *"Prudentia plus importat quam scientia practica:
nam ad scientiam practicam pertinet universale
iudicium de agendis; sicut fornicationem esse
malam, furtum non esse faciendum et huiusmodi.
Qua quidem scientia existente, in particulari actu
continget iudicium rationis intercipi, ut non recte
diiudicet; et propter hoc dicitur parum valere ad*

virtutem, quia ea existente contingit hominem con-
tra virtutem peccare. Sed ad prudentiam pertinet
recte iudicare de singulis agibilibus, prout sint nunc
agenda: quod quidem iudicium corrumpitur per
quodlibet peccatum. Et ideo prudentia manente
homo non peccat; unde ipsa non parum, sed multum
confert ad virtutem; immo ipsam virtutem causat."
Virt. comm. 6 ad 1.

23 First, St. Thomas's concept of "art" does not mean
primarily, as is the case today, the whole realm
of artistic creation and of artistic products, but
rather the inner attitude of the artist himself, by
virtue of which he creates. Secondly, *ars* embraces
both the realm of art proper and the realm of technical science. The shaping of an artifact according to certain "rules" is, to Thomas, the common
element of art and technical science; there are no
less plain standards for the "structure" of a sonnet
and for the construction of a ship or a bridge. It
is clear that the concept of *ars* in this sense is specifically medieval (and perhaps also specifically
characteristic of Romance languages and thought).
Cf. i. a. I, II, 57, 4.

24 *"Les manières d'être prudent, d'être moral, se re-*
nouvellent et se multiplient à l'infini, étant donnés
l'instabilité et la variété des circonstances de la vie
pratique; et pourtant, partout et toujours, nous
sommes obligés d'être vertueux et de servir Dieu.
La fin de l'art étant particulière et restreinte, l'artisan
a, pour ainsi dire, la carte forcée dans le choix de

ses moyens; du moins la variété de ces moyens n'est pas de rigueur: il suffit que ceux employés habituellement servent a réussir le type d'oeuvre que l'on a en vue. Il y a du procédé au fond de toute technique, et la science technique est précisément la science des meilleurs procédés. Il n'y a pas de procédés ne varietur *en morale: la prudence vertueuse doit accomoder son discernement à l'instabilité des circonstances changeantes de la vie pratique. Pour autant qu'il tendrait à se fixer, le discernement se rapprocherait du procédé. La casuistique, poussée à l'excès, substitue des procédés et des recettes à l'infinie souplesse que doit garder la prudence vertueuse en face des complexités de la vie morale."* H. D. Noble, O.P., in his above-mentioned commentary on the *Quaestiones on Prudence* in the French edition of the *Summa Theologica* (Paris, 1925), p. 238.

25 Paul Claudel, *L'Otage.*

26 *"Si la théologie morale était ramenée à la casuistique . . . elle deviendrait la science des péchés à éviter plutôt que celle des vertus à exercer et à parfaire."* Garrigou-Lagrange, "Du Caractère métaphysique de la théologie morale de Saint Thomas." *Revue thomiste,* vol. 8 (1925), p. 342.

27 Linsenmann, "Untersuchungen über die Lehre von Gesetz und Freiheit." *Theologische Quartalsschrift.* Tübingen, vol. 53 (1871), p. 238. "Entangled in such a Talmudistic spirit of pedantry, a man can scarcely take a step without his father confessor."—

J. B. Hirscher, *Über das Verhältnis des Evangeliums zu der theologischen Scholastik der neuesten Zeit im katholischen Deutschland.* Tübingen, 1823, p. 238. In an outstanding treatise by P. Daniel Feuling, O.S.B., concerning prudence (which he denotes by an older word, *discretio*), he writes the following encouraging sentence: "Is there not among us a widespread tendency, though unconfessed, aimed at 'preserving' maturing and mature—perhaps we should do better to say, physically adult persons —as far as possible from making their own moral judgments and independent decisions of conscience? Are not general rules established (and we are not speaking here of their establishment and legislation by the proper authorities) concerning moral actions and moral life in the most diverse fields, rules which everyone is supposed to observe, rules which are intended to determine down to detail, and often down to triviality, what the moral order demands; rules which are then straightway equated with this moral order? And are we not at times inclined, and moreover quite ready, to raise the severe charge of immoral thinking and actions against those who balk at *such* casuistry and adhere to the great and fundamental moral truth that virtue lies in the mean, but not in an abstract, levelling mean, rather in the mean according to the circumstances, conditions, spiritual states, principles, and above all according to the person acting? It is really not surprising that given such tutelage and such in-

fluences, the indispensable practice in the virtue of
distinguishing and deciding according to circumstances, and therefore according to the real moral
laws, is more or less omitted; and that, moreover,
virtually all moral courage to make independent
moral decisions is undermined, and often lost entirely. In such a situation it is inevitable that many
a less stanch soul grows despondent, confronts the
moral life with helplessness and perplexity, and
gives way to despair unless he finds a truly discreet
person of firm judgment to give counsel and aid
with his scruples. To combat these grave evils there
is only *one* aid: persevering tutelage and training
in *discretio*." P. Daniel Feuling, O.S.B., "Discretio."
Benediktinische Monatsschrift, vol. 7 (1925), pp.
359 f.

4

1 Ver. 14, 6.
2 II, II, 47, 13 ad 2.
3 I, II, 18, 5.
4 Cf. *Die Wirklichkeit und das Gute,* pp. 52 ff., on
the structure of moral "total action."
5 *"Prudentia praecise dirigit in his quae sunt ad finem.
. . . Sed finis agibilium praeexistit in nobis dupli-
citer: scil. per cognitionem naturalem de fine hominis [synderesis!]; . . . alio modo quantum ad
affectionem: et sic fines agibilium sunt in nobis per
virtutes morales. . . . Ad prudentiam requiruntur*

et intellectus finium et virtutes morales, quibus affectus recte collocatur in fine; et propter hoc oportet omnem prudentem virtuosum esse." Ver. 5, 1.

6 "How this inner penetration of practical cognition and its reflection, judging and deciding [by the will; J. P.], takes place, is a question that touches upon mysteries. But this mystery is experienced reality and the condition of all morality, and we may well say that in its character of a mystery, light is cast upon it by the metaphysical nature of the mind. For as cognition the mind is directed toward all being, including action and its moral determinants; and as will the mind is directed toward all good, including the goodness of cognition, especially that aspect of cognition which is of practical importance. This directing springs from the ultimate depths of the mind's being and nature." P. Daniel Feuling, O.S.B., "Discretio." *Benediktinische Monatsschrift,* vol. 7 (1925), p. 256.

7 "*Ad actum virtutis requiritur, quod sit rectus et quod sit voluntarius. Sed sicut voluntarii actus principium est voluntas, ita recti actus principium est ratio.*" Ver. 14, 5, obj. 11.

8 Cf. *Die Wirklichkeit und das Gute,* p. 109.

9 Virt. card. 2.

10 Ver. 27, 5 ad 5.

11 Ver. 14, 5 ad 11.

12 II, II, 52, 2.

13 II, II, 52, 2 ad 3.

14 II, II, 52, 2 ad 1.
15 *De sermone Domini in monte,* cap. 4.
16 II, II, 52, 4.
17 I, II, 61, 5.